Love,

Thy Soul

♥

Dedication

This is for all the times that you tripped
on your words and bit your tongue;
For every time your voice cracked.
This is for when the words escaped you,
stealing your breath, and for every
expression they tried to attack.

This is for when you
swallowed your words;
For them to never digest.
This is for the voiceless
screams and shrieks;
unintentionally suppressed.

This is for your locked
jaw and tense tongue;
For the silence that
consumed your soul.
This is for the suppressed
and the repressed.

It is time for
your story
to be told.

♥

chapters

♥

The Fool

My karma, I accept, universe.
Here are my confessions. It is
time to sit and face this cold
depression; Time to feel
every repression
etched within this
broken and
weary
soul.

Don't you know who you are?
Of the light you bring to this world
and the erratic beauty within your soul?
Don't you know who you are?

Do not scoff at me!
Do not try to hide,
For I see your essence
Residing inside.

You asked for help,
Now here I am.
Just take my hand.

- The Universe

They would not let go from the bondage.
For they were too comforted,
In the hug they gave themselves.
Realizing they were not alone in the world.
They had their higher self.

Erasing my disgrace
Wiping clean my tear filled face
My love for me - somewhere misplaced
Needing to heal my heart and fill it with grace
For Self
Love.

You might not be prepared
You might get scared
You might try to hide
The Universe
is by your side
No need
to feel
despaired

Love,
Thy Soul

To love myself, I have to find a way.
I am alive for my son,
To make him smile. Every single day.
To love myself, I have to find a way.
Even on the days that are gray
And there is no sun.
To love myself, I have to find a way.
I remain alive for my son.

Let my happiness be his gym
where he can explore and have fun.
I don't want my happiness to depend on him.
Let my happiness be his gym.
Let it fill his cup to the rim.
I heal for my son.
Let my happiness be his gym
where he can explore and have fun.

May my love be what he remembers me by.
This is my biggest desire inside.
Even if he sees me cry,
May my love be what he remembers me by;
and that on me he can rely.
May my love be what he remembers me by.
This is my biggest desire inside.

Please
gift me
challenges
so that I may
grow, learn, and release.

Allow me, universe
To become your masterpiece
Mold me, shape me, and nourish me;
Teach me to learn how to master peace.
I'm ready for who you need me to be...

Love,
  and peace

<u>A Talk In The Mirror</u>

I know you are scared but take a look.
Look at yourself in the mirror.
Take a look at those piercing
yet tender eyes and those
wrinkles made of smiles.
Look at the way
your hair falls
on your
face.

Fairly misplaced, yet perfectly placed.
Do not let intrusive thoughts take
control. Let these thoughts all go.
Keep your gaze on your eyes
and do not let go.
Now look at your
shadow straight
in the
eye

...and kill it with love and compassion.
I know you want to banish it-
Send it straight to hell. But it
won't be long before its
Back pulling you down
into your shell.

You're now safe.
Time to
Heal.

Dissolve the darkness with love and grace.
It has been your worst enemy
That, you can't erase. It's time
to make it your best friend.
Make love where you see
Pain and love with
Yourself you'll
attain
Love,

Thy Soul

The karma we have accumulated, we can't offset.
Learn from your lessons but never forget.
We can make mistakes and still live without regrets
If we live purely from the heart.
If we clear our damaging mindsets.
Go on darling, melt your samskaras
and watch the sunset.

        - The Universe

Eye AM my own healer
with every emotional wound
Eye heal, life is bestowed upon me

Love,
Thy Soul

cansada de ser.
Sick and tired of feeling sick.
It is time to live.

-    Hypothyroidism can suck my....

Standing up, after every last fall
Despite your dark inner battles,
Being kind of an oddball,
Or societal rules,
Neither big or small.
Eye admire you;
Scared and all.
Now, stand
tall.

-   The Universe

She is beautiful,
doused in self rejection.
She needs to let go
and believe once more;
That magic is alive
and that there are kind souls.
That we can all change
ourselves from the inside.
That her soul
does not need
to hide.

Love,
Thy Soul

Universe,
I trust you to lead me;
To put in my path what is needed...
To allow the course of best healing.
Universe, I feel the changes within me.
Please help me heal to the best degree.

Synchronicity is ever present.
Allow it to make you surprised.
The more you find them, the more they frequent.
Your love for me will be hypnotized.

- The Universe

Stop resisting
The universe is ready for you
Stop fighting
The earth lives for you
Stop pretending
that you are so small
Stop believing
that you don't belong

You are worthy... Tall or short
You matter... That you can't distort
The universe's love for you, you can't abort
It's there to guide, and to give you support

We all have our own path to take
We don't need a highway
Just live and wander
Dare to take the scenic route
Drift off to nowhere and
find yourself a little astray
Get lost in nature or
dreams inside your head
Perhaps, we will see each other
somewhere along the way

Love,
Thy Soul

When negative thoughts of self come
to mind, look in the mirror and give yourself a
compliment
Three times

Compliment your heart and your soul
Your body, your mind, your insecurities
Your body
Listens

Allow yourself to shine like
a mother fucking star
we are all a bit weird
You aren't that bizarre
even if you're a little odd
can't you see, that's what
makes you who you are

The thing about the experience
of being human is that you're
always connected; Always
intertwined. Someone out
there has the same odd
habits; wishing
upon the
same old
star

Love,
Thy Soul

crackling gravel below my numb feet;
comforting. Gentle sounds cracking
open memories of my
Distant childhood home;
once upon a time.
Simplicities
of walking
on dirt
roads.

- con amor

- *You call Me*

Gringa: Erasing my culture
from my blood. Foreigner: As if I didn't live
Here most of
my life.

Hairy: You call me while wearing
your hair extensions and eyebrow fills. Fat: As if
It were an
insult.

Sana Sana

Potito de marijuana

A little cream, un poquito de pomada

No me llames Dolores

Gordita tampoco

Lazy is an insult to mi perfeccionismo

It's not just the pain

Si no mi alma

Heal me today, si no mañana

They tell me,

"Just be yourself. You ain't gotta change."
They just want me to stay the same.
I've barely even let out the strange.

My being, undeclared.
I've barely been me.
Always too shy,
Always scared
to be...
Me.

Oh,
I can
Not do that!
I can't do this!
All I want is for
my body to feel bliss.

I can not be a cliché,
you see. Please, do not let me drown
in another's reflection of me.

Broke free from others' definitions;
Time to focus on my own strengths
And my own earthly missions.
I am not an actress
Just out of practice
in what it means
to truly be
myself.

Magical trees breaking through rocks;
A temporary permanence.
A symbol of resilience.
Perhaps it was destiny that
it had to rise and overcome;
A testament, that one can thrive
In a state that is cumbersome.

Love,
Thy Soul

Love handles and loose skin
wrinkles and stretch marks
Storage of experience
Marks of existence
Traces of miracles
Stripes of love
Your skin

Embrace
Your vessel

Love,
Thy Soul

People love in different ways
People live in different ways
People heal in different ways
People grieve in different ways

There is no right way
There is only a wrong way
For our own present circumstance
Everything else is just a test
An infinite test of the soul
To find what works

To live the unexpressed
Until our soul is undressed
Until we become our essence
Then we are birthed, all over again

Love,
Thy Soul

They say grow where you are planted
but some of us are
the wind

Love,
Thy Soul

Everytime you breathe,
You breathe me;
You breathe you.
Breathe.

I write...
To clear away the program
That makes me feel like a sham
Put in by those who didn't give a damn
To remember who the fuck I AM
I write.

The mind can be a
fascinating instrument
Do you not agree
It is interesting how
we are all programmed to see
To witness our past
experiences happening
right before our eyes
Diverse perspectives of life
over and over
As if it were memorized

Love,
Thy Soul

You
do not
always have
to be scared of
the rain and the storm

Dare to dance in the rain
Dare to dare a little more
Keep doing things out of the norm
Feel the energy. Become the storm

Dare to exceed your expectations
Dare to feel the power of your spirit
Bend your understanding of physics
With the storm, become intimate

Dance in sync with the rain...Find
your calm in your bones... calm
the storm, with your love.

Go on darling
Remember
who you
are

Love,
Thy Soul

He
will have
his own voice.
He'll have his own
way.

He
will be
freethinking
And be loved for
it.

I
dislike
standing up
for myself or
upsetting those dear
to me, but when it comes
to protecting my child, I
will not budge and I will not plead.
I will raise him as I fucking please.
Universe, guide me to become
Better than the mother he needs.
Give me patience. Gift me peace.
He needs a parent that
will guide him, not lead.
May my dreams of
parenthood
become
real.

when you aren't
looking for purpose
purpose finds you
A conspiracy of the universe
gifting you what you sincerely desire
even if you don't yet know it to be true

Love,
Thy Soul

Don't
fit into
their little boxes
You're so many things

mosaic
Infinite
yet minuscule

Heavy as love
Light, as air

Love,
Thy Soul

Alternate dimensions through space and time
Being opened in the back of my mind
Making their way into my reality;
Exploring my dimensionality.
Past lives in my dreams
Where eye lived in the woods, or so it seems.
No ordinary woods, the trees were our home.
The forest, our neighborhood where we were
Free, secure, and happy to thrill and roam.

Love,
Thy Soul

cravings...
Do you ignore them and bid them goodbye?
Restricting

cravings...
Do you give in and devour what you're tempting?
Do you decide to take little nibbles, sigh?

cravings...
Don't ignore them or bid them goodbye.

To savor every bite until your temptation craves you?
A submissive or a temptress?
Oh, we're not talking about food; well maybe that, too.

Savor every bite until your temptation craves you.
Or are you too timid to feel "ahhh" and "ooohhh."
It's time for pleasure to no longer suppress
Savor every bite until your temptation craves you.
A submissive or a temptress?

The same goes for food, Eye suppose.
May you shine with an after sex
and a happy tummy glow.

Dancing to the peace radiating within
Un baile del corazón y alma
Surrendering to the vibrations
A mild trance hypnotization
Brought on by meditation
Their minds wander off and
Drift away and they
Float along to
The pulse of
Their peace
Song

Love,
Thy Soul

There's so much to see
So many things yet to do
Those who are wise would
advise you to stop and think
Think with your brain and
follow your own two damn feet
Open your soft heart
Skip to it's magical beat

Love,
Thy Soul

Judgement

Stuck
In cold
solitude,
Bathed in my tears;
Living my worst fears.
Heart, undervalued and
Gasping··· for a string of hope
That life does not have to be this
Depressing. I don't have to spend my
Life distressing if I stop suppressing
These old wounds.

Find yourself lost
in the middle of the trees.
Find an unbeaten path,
and follow the breeze.
Let your soul wander,
allow it to be pleased.
Then allow it to heal,
by bathing in the seas.

-The Universe

Pain can be limiting
to our human existence
So are our beliefs
It's time to rewonder
limits to find some relief

Love,
Thy Soul

When all of a sudden
Synchronicities are hard
To understand or explain
Yes, it is all happening
cosmic entertain
It's just part of the matrix
Fear: try to abstain
Ascended masters are near

-    The Universe

Some days Eye cannot
seem to write and then Eye go
live and words become alive.

When there are no words,
healing has arrived and when
there are words, life is revived.

The illnesses of the body
may change your dreams
but never your soul

Love,
Thy Soul

Writing, my expression
Wild hair, my essence
Dance, my freedom
Music, my therapy
Magic, my life
Love,
My Soul

Eye am the beat of the drum
beating through my varicose veins.

A voluntary reckoning
with a foreign ego··· Eye let go
of my control and desires
and watch the music take over.

Unstoppable force of rhythm
permeating through my vessel,
making their way into a flow
of expressive existence.

Eye am no one. Eye am everyone.
Awakening. Raising energy.

Eye am one with the vibrations;
Becoming my higher self.

Love,
Thy Soul

Lately, Eye find myself in
everyone and everything.
Microscopic cells scattered
throughout this vast universe.
An invisible attempt
To make some kind of sense of
what it is to be human.

Oh, but what is
quantum entanglement but
invisible connection
of souls through souls?

Love,
Thy Soul

Eye know you get tired
That you want to quit;
cast yourself aside.
Eye know it's easy
To feel weak, fatigued,
and dissatisfied.
Jot down all your
insecurities,
Your disappointments,
And your unmet needs;
All of your perceived
incapabilities.
Let's burn them away
On this New Moon's night,
As we focus on our
intentions and plant
seeds of nourishment,
Self love, and delight.

- The Universe

children teach us
the way of the heart
That we have an inner
child within us all

Perhaps it's a bit cranky
and needs a long nap
Perhaps it likes to
bounce off the walls
Or skip down the hall

It's time to spend some
time outdoors this fall
Time to run, slip, and slide
To dance in the rainfall
Adulthood, override

Love,
Thy Soul

There is something
about the sunset
How all of the colors
can calm your mindset
The beautiful
effect of chemicals
Sprayed above our heads
It is all just
fucking comical

What is eating you up
Is it remorse, or is it guilt
It's time to tell the truth
to whom you've done wrong
Please, do not let your
precious soul wilt

Go on, be sincere
It's time to be strong
To be cruel, your heart
was not built
There is no
procrastinating
This can not be prolonged

Love,
Thy Soul

I hate how much this hurts;
waiting for the best,
Expecting the worst.
I feel like my heart
has been cursed,
Still, I give,
No love needed
reimbursed.

To be forgiven
Is a powerful medicine
That is priceless

To forgive oneself
Is a potent medicine
Worthy of your soul

Many cannot afford either...

When pain comes to visit,
it's time to open the door.
When pain comes to visit,
it is time to make some tea.
When pain comes to visit,
It is time to grieve.
When pain comes to visit,
it is time to feel.
When pain comes to visit,
it's time to empty yourself.
When pain comes to visit,
It's inevitable.
When pain comes to visit,
love yourself a little more.
When pain comes to visit,
make sure to take extra
good care of your soul.

- The Universe

If rainbows could talk
They would speak
of your magic

If water could speak
It would tell you to
Surrender into yourself

If La Luna communicated
With you, she would
Simply listen

If your soul spoke
What would it say?

wandering thoughts can
linger, nibbling on your mind
Eye know it is not
easy becoming aligned
You do not need to
rationalize all of the
unwanted thoughts that
Make their way into your head
It does not always
Pay off over digesting
Or thinking ahead
Sometimes letting go can mean
losing your damn mind
and take chances to watch your
Precious soul unbind

Love,
Thy Soul

Go on, darling. Breathe.
Exhale or let out a gasp;
All that's lying beneath.

Go on, darling. Breathe.
Vomit out your inner crap.
So much lying underneath.

Go on and breathe, darling.
Life inhaled with every breath.
Sweetie, your lungs are starving.

– The Universe

444
There is unconditional love,
support, and protection
at your door.
allow yourself to feel
It at your core.

Look for the signs, darling;
Left by anonymous.
They're showing you the way.

You say that you want
to find happiness
But you keep resisting
My love for you, sweetie

can you not see that
your pain is screaming
waiting for emptiness
Of no more resistance

Allow in all the love
Already residing
within your sacred bones.

I can not make you feel
worthy of what is
already yours.

- The universe

There is something mesmerizing
about the ocean pulling you in.
It will hypnotize you just enough
to bring you to it's shore.
The roars of the waves and
aroma of the salty air
are usually enough to
allow the healing to begin.
Perhaps stick your feet in,
or take a little dip.
The ocean is a
dangerous
piece of art,
with the power to make
anyone drown or fall in love.
It will definitely take your
breath away
in all the right ways.
The ocean understands
your emotions and
never judges your soul.
Go on, float and you will feel
the heartbeat.
Poseidon likes to calm your soul,
while drowning all the demons
attacking your heart.
A misunderstood masterpiece
gifting peace.
My dear
old love.

It's time for endings
And fresh beginnings
For our hearts to heal
For our pain to feel
So our egos can kneel
And our soul be revealed

Love,
Thy Soul

The Sun

This is when we make love
To ourselves intimately,
Seduce our doubts, and
cuddle with our fears;
Lust for our genuine smile,
Date our dreams,
court our inhibitions,
And hug our numbness.

This is when we
marry our self-esteem.
Let's put our own selves
on a pedestal.
And grow our wings.
For we are eternal,
And we will do as
we damn well please.

Explore the *flavor* of life
with your **taste** buds
Fill your **eyes** with
the *colors* of the rainbow
Entice your **nose**
with new *aromas*
Listen to the *music*
of the universe
Allow life to ***touch***
Your tender heart

Love,
Thy Soul

Climaxing with my
higher self connection
Brought on by this
mercy of ascension
Bathing in the
Pulsating sensations
of unconditional
Imperfect perfection
The gift of love
and divine protection
Eye AM healing my being
with affirmations
Letting go of all my
perceived imperfections
Dancing to the beat
without prejudice
of my midsection
I'm finding time slows
and speeds up at diverse
accelerations.

Allow yourself to be
A perfectly imperfect
chaotic melody
A song of the universe
Roaming aimlessly
Imperfectly perfect
You deserve
Your full respect

Love,
Thy Soul

Eye am you
You are me

Living life
Separately

Perceptions

alternately

Meeting
each other
Infinitely

So you can
be you
and Eye
can be
me

A romance with yourself
is what you need if
you are single, wife,
or groom to be.
Look in the mirror,
what do you see?

Write it down and
read it to thee.
Does it sweep you
off of your feet?
Or is it something
you would never
even say discreet?

Change your view,
change your focus.
Shed away all of
the hocus pocus.

No shame, no pouts.
You are perfect;
Inside, and out.

The Universe

Look in the mirror again.
What do you see?
A glimmer of magic
in the making.
Look at your soul
sparkling inside.
Enough to make your
fears run and hide.

Love,
Thy Soul

Our spiritual essence
of love

Pumping through the cosmos
Through darkness and light
Through nebulas and the voids

The heart of the universe
Pumping through me

Thump, thump
Pumping through you
Thump, thump
Pumping

A cosmic dance
of love

Drumming
Thump. Thump
Go on, and dance
Go on, and heal

The clover of
The mind, body
heart, and soul

Love,
Thy Soul

Two of me
Me in two
Old me, new me
Dark vs light
Sick vs healthy
Sad vs happy

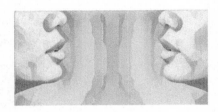

Ego self and higher self
contrasting personality
of yin and yang
Life interpretations
Through dreams...
Amnesty

Then, who am I?

what is magic, but the music
of nature whispering
to your soul?

what is magic, but sand
swallowing you in as
the waves reach your feet?

what is magic, but the moon
and the sun greeting you
at the same time?

what is magic, but the wiff
of a homemade meal?

what is magic, but the buzzing
of dragonflies swarming nearby?

what is magic, but the sound
of a heartbeat you love?

what is magic...
but pure love?

She laid awake,
with her fingers running
slowly through her
warm delicate skin.
Scrolling through words
written in sin.

Enticing her body,
with gentle caresses.
She craved to be devoured.
Her mind raced,
surely empowered.

Deep in imagination,
She teased her inner thigh.
Raising her energy,
She was all the wise.

Blood pooling on her soft lips,
with a tender gasp of pleasure.
For these sweet little moments,
She surely does treasure.

Eye believe in the universe
and Eye believe in me
Eye don't want to believe,
Eye want to experience.
And feel the magical
brilliance
Of being
hueman

Love,
Thy Soul

Look at those wrinkles
They speak of your full life
Your experience
Your existence
Written with love
on your skin
Kiss your precious hands
and touch your dear lines
Allow your love of self to align
Just remember, darling
My love for you is genuine

– The Universe

The Universe, my lover
Gaia, my healer
The Sun, my admirer
The trees are my roots
The wind is my companion
The moon, my therapist
The ocean is my alchemist
Nature is my medicine
Kindness is my weakness
My higher self, my guru
Soul, my guide
Love,
My soul

Remembering things that
I don't want to remember.
Memories deliberately
erased from my mind.
How could I have
Forgotten so much time?

Conversing with memories
over a cup of tea,
It is time to set them free.

A ceremonial death.
I set fire to my woes,
Dark memories
Burned to ashes.

Essence evaporated.
Transformed
Into freedom,
no wings needed.
I become the breath,
I lost long ago.

check in with yourself, darling.
How is your vessel feeling?
Is it alive, yet serene?
Or do you feel as if you are
in need of some morphine?

How is your mind these days?
Eye hope it is well fed and satisfied.
Are your mental tabs full to the rim?
Place your negative thoughts
into the recycle bin.

How are your emotions doing?
Well balanced, on the outside, it seems.
Any constipated feelings
that need to be shit out?
Or an explosive shitstorm
You have been trying not to blowout?

Gaea and Earth.
One heals us and the other poisons us.
One, we wander: one, we are slaves.
One, we worship; one, we degrade.
One, we nurture; one, we destroy.
One, we call home; one, we rent.
One will survive; one, will end.

Do not mold me, Universe
Take me as I am
Embrace your creation
Of this stubborn spirit
Do not mold me, Universe
Show me that I am
Not unacceptable
That I am not a mistake

Dancing to my own beat
Spinning in and out of place
While looking at the sky
Filling my heart with glee
Rising energy
through every part of me
One with source
my soul becomes free
changing the chemistry
of my being
making me carefree
When tranced by dancing
Eye let go of all my anxieties

Love,
Thy Soul

"know thyself"

You think that
you know yourself
But it is time
to stop self deceit
You are forever
changing
A kaleidoscope
oh so neat
Always expanding
or dissolving
Alternating through
dimensions
Evolving
There is always
Something
new to learn
something yet
to be discovered
at every turn
A little glimmer
a new glow
You have yet
to get to know

Love,
Thy Soul

Karma already exists, sweetheart.
You don't have to punish yourself.
Learn the lessons and listen
to your higher self.

- The Universe

The unseen will see
The silence listens
The wind likes to speak
The moon always knows
And the fucking sun
Does not give a fuck
Who it is blinding

Synching with the skies, the mind thrives.
Synching with water, the heart breathes.
Synching with the sun, the soul shines.
Synching with music, the body is free.

Love,
Thy Soul

Healing comes in waves,
It's always washing us clean.
You will float easier when
It is willingly.
close your eyes, open your heart,
and take synching breaths.
watch your rhythm become one
with the currency.
Las olas de mi alma...

To be the best version of you,
Imagine what that is to be true. Dare to dream big.
Nothing's too
Taboo.

Your soul, don't undervalue.
You are worthy, no matter what you've been through; in
all that you
Pursue.

– The Universe

Universe, I thought
I was done chasing after love.
Only to keep catching myself
Back in the starting position;
Like a looped race track.
Universe, I don't want a race.
can we dance instead?

    -   con amor

Just tell me what you want...
For me to run and hide?
Are you scared of the power
beating out of my heart?
Are you waiting for me
to tear my life apart?
Go on and watch the show.
Eye will dress myself in love
And change the world
before your eyes.
Eye will transform your
wickedness into magick
with my love and light.

Love,

This life...
is about love
To cloak the world
in all shades
of love

Love,
Thy Soul

He looked into her eyes, and
caressed her rosy cheeks.
He placed a strand of hair,
gently behind her ear.
So simple, yet so cliche.
No fear. No worries. No dismay.

Locked into his eyes,
she longed for a passionate kiss.
She let out a tear, instead;
slowly dripping down her delicate face.

He kissed her forehead, and whispered,
"Babygirl, I'm here."
He wiped away her sorrows,
and pulled her near.

He said,
"The world is mad. Mad you hear?
But right here. Here, you are you...
And I am me.

And we are as perfect, as perfect as can be.
Let me hold you near. And we will make love...
Make love straight out of fear."

She laid on his heart, emerging
with the warmth of his body.
Bathing in serenity and comfortable silence.

She whispered in his ear, "Thank you for being here,"
sending tingles of shivers up his spine.

He took her hand; fingers intertwined.
comforted her with another kiss on top of her head, genuine.

He couldn't take his eyes off of her;
Further thought that if he closed his eyes,
it would have just been visions of her.

He caressed her
and cuddled her tight.
"Darling, I've got you.
Even if it's just for the night."

Perhaps if she could just see the light
residing within her, the world would be
just that much more infatuating.

She gently kissed his cheek, and muddled into a dream.
He did not know what he had just done for her.
He gave her a safe space and asked nothing of her.

She woke up alone, yet feeling reassured
that her divine love lives somewhere inside of her.

I am **him.**
I am **her**.
I am **whole** on my own.

I can not give up on the idea of love,
for I have felt it deep within my soul.
For now I'll just love me anyway, anyhow.
I'll love myself completely affectionately.
Someway, somehow.

Do not wait for the afterlife;
for heaven or hell.
Hell and heaven are what we think they are,
just like life itself.

There is no avoiding pain in this matrix.
What is the point, afterall,
To spend life without feeling,
or taking a chance at all.

Fuck finding yourself
Eye am remembering
myself
Eye AM allowing
myself to grow
exponentially
No barriers or
restrictions
My soul has
demanded
liberation
My self
your masterpiece
in creation

Love,
Thy Soul

"Love yourself first"

As if it has some sort of end,
Some sort of trophy,
A degree, or worse,
a trend.

Self love might be a journey
But let's not pretend
That we don't all love
To hate ourselves,
without intend.

we are all here
to heal our souls.
No ifs ands or buts;
There are no loopholes.

We are eternal magic.
Life gets tragic,
Nevertheless.

So keep on loving,
But allow love in
So that you can
liberate the love
You carry within.

My smile, a white flag
of unconscious self defence.
"Please do not hurt me"
Peeled off: pure tension expressed;
Nothing but a fearful plea.

They watch from above
When their intrusive thoughts
bring out my cries
They watch from above
Every time Eye rise
Eye do not care
about being watched
You, watching from above
Enjoy the goddamn show
Even you eye will surprise

Life is a journey
with no end in sight
Some may see the future
Other's see the past
Some are terrified of the dark
Others are scared of their light
At some point in time
we are all outcasts
All of us, finding ourselves
through the twilight
While we may be miniscule
our presence is vast
Don't be afraid to exist, darling
It's your fucking birthright

Love,
Thy Soul

No matter how much
Eye try to love myself
Loving myself means
admitting to thouself
This sincere hunger
For love

Love,
Thy Self

❤

The Tower

Free will
rings
the security
alarm
of the matrix.
Proceed
at your own
accord.

Seduce my heart with your actions.
Make love to my ego with your passion.
Dance with my soul with your mind.
Quiet my mind with your heart.
Liberate my body with your ego.
Taste my magic with your soul.

I wish I had known back then, that
There is no such thing as running away,
when time tends to lapse in your brain.
Perhaps, I would have still chosen to
Disappear that day.

Now I welcome the
screams and memories
but they will not overstay.
Gratefully binded to the promise
I had made to thyself
to give my child(ren) a better childhood
that I could ever wanted for myself.

I gathered the courage to look at myself.

To look at my blemishes.

MY dark circles. My stomach pouch.

Humbled with life.

MY stretchmarks on my breast.

MY full, bushy eyebrows slightly connecting in between.

Signs of life.

The waves of MY hips.

MY dimples and cellulite on MY ass

I never even looked at before.

MY hair growing underneath MY chin.

My wild hair, with it's own life.

Unconditional love.

MY hair growing all over MY body.

MY short stature.

Perfectly imperfectly me.

MY smile. The light in MY eyes.

The life bursting in MY face.

A stranger I love.

MY curves of MY waist.

MY confidence. Sexy.

MY vessel. MY mind.

Body Reclaimed.

MY heart. MY soul.

Acceptance and encouragement.

Support and love.

Proud in the mirror.

Who knew that was possible.

Who am I?

Oh, yeah.

I AM love.

When you radiate with light,
people gravitate towards you.
Be careful when your fire
accidently burns out.
Some people only seeked light
instead of feeling the
warmth coming from your heart.
If you are lucky enough,
perhaps some will stay to
help relight your fire.

-The Universe

In the midst of trees
Sitting whistling to birds
An intimate connection
Lost in trance of sweet serenity
Magic is nature
Nature, I AM
Synching as one
I lose myself
Breathing in sunshine
Exhaling blue
Making my wish
Of clear skies come true.
I find myself
Dancing to the beat
Of the branches of the trees
Accessing alternate dimensions
Through transcendental movement
A misplaced child of nature
Remembering myself
Becoming myself
Being
My higher self.

Let people assume
Let people believe
Get them to wonder
Soon enough they will see
All of that you can achieve
Reflect their magic
Provide the spark
So they can be all
That they can be.

    - The Universe

People are mirrors
If you judge me, you are judging you
Eye have to blame me if I blame you
If you love me, you really love you
That is always true

It is a little more complicated than that
Some mirrors are woefully cracked.
Some are odd carnival mirrors.
And some are tinted black,
Making a window
To the soul.

Intersectantly living
In each other's matrix
We don't see what we want
We see what we need to experience
Eye call it cosmic internal directions
What you perceive when you don't see

Don't feel guilty for smiling when there is goodness around.
It's not always depression that keeps us so down.
Sometimes it's those we hold dear.
Sometimes it is our own fear.

Sometimes it is the passive aggressive shame
that we have absorbed through the years
Sometimes it is because we deprive
ourselves, from the ability to thrive.

Learn to follow your intuition and follow your heart.
Allow the goodness in, and the negative to depart.
Darling, will you allow the life meant for you to start?

-The Universe

Beauty is not something you look at
It is something that you can feel

when love and sincerity
take over and when things
are exquisitely
and painfully
fucking real

Beauty
is
your caged
soul tasting
sweet liberty

Beauty isn't pretty
but it is always real

There is beauty everywhere
See with your heart, just look and see

can you let life touch your tender heart
Life: what a painful, beautiful, masterpiece

Love,
Thy Soul

you feel like you deserve all of the bad that you
have gone through, you deserve all the good coming, too.
Don't punish yourself for the bad and then
do the same with the good.
Relearn gratitude.

-The Universe

I used to be afraid of having an ego,
until I made love to mine...

You do not
Have to win
Battles if
You do not
Fight their wars
Instead, make love

Love,
Thy Soul

Healing is a seedling that must be
watered, or it will eventually wilt

Some seedlings turn into trees
Standing strong against the change of winds

Some seedlings turn into plants, of all sorts
Some seedlings are weeds that multiply across lawns
An unstoppable force, knowing no boundaries

Some become strong, some survive
Some have the capacity to revive
Make sure to care for your garden
And fill it with love

Water the seedlings with your love and compassion
Fertilize them with your honest loving intentions
Keep any bugs away that is harming it's growth
It must be nurtured, it must grow

The seedlings of healing
Will bloom and cause you to glow

Love
Thy Soul

Don't seek
Just be
Be bamboo
Be a fucking tree

Love,
Thy Soul

Dear Universe,

I just want to be happy
Make a little dance
Do a little spin
Take a chance

I know what I have to do
Choose love over fear
And make myself
my own muse

Love,
Thy Soul

You are allowed to doubt reality
Just as you are allowed to doubt magic
This is the way of the mystic
Don't lose your curiosity

-    The Universe

continue to live your life
don't be afraid to pursue
All of your goals
even if they seem
a bit taboo

Try a handstand
Put on a tutu
Make sure that
your dreams
you outdo

Be your own cheerleader
Be your own guru
Stroll in the woods
write a haiku
Why don't you take
a chance or two

Love,
Thy Soul

Have you stopped, and
taken care of yourself?
Have you *nourished*, and
made sure to feed your tummy?

Have you *paused*, and
checked on your breathing?
Have you *breathed*, and
released what no longer serves?

Have you *dreamed*, and
found a way to laugh?
Have you *meditated*, and
looked at a sunset?

Have you *lived*, and
danced in the rain?
Have you *explored*, and
smiled at a flower?

Have you *opened up*, and
shared your love?
Have you *loved*, and
hugged a tree?
Have you *stopped*,
and lived life?

Love,
Thy Soul

A time comes to learn
How to stand up for yourself;
Learn how to toughen up.
Sometimes you need
to be a bitch
It's okay,
just not
for fun.

They
Say you
can't live a
Sweet life if you're
Bitter.

I
Guess they
Have never tasted
The magical synergy of
bittersweetness.

You know you're **healing**
Not when you are *healthy*
But when you're **living**

You know you're **living**
Not when you are *doing*
But when you're **being**

You know you are **being**
Not when you do not *do*
But when what you do
Is **true to you**

You know you are **healed**
When being you is
All the *medicine* your soul needs
When you allow your
Soul to lead

Soon, it will be time
to grow your spine.
To use your voice
To clear the dust off
and shine

— The universe

You can trust the process,
And still complain.
Yet, is it really complaining
If you are stating reality?
Or are you accepting the circumstance
That needs to be changed?
Go ahead and heal
Everything is real,
Just as everything ain't.

Imagine life if you were a tree
Living your days happily
Until the woodchoppers come
They take, and take, and then take some
Inevitable karma
Hopefully your afterlife
Lives and gives warmth in the shape of
a house, that transforms into
a home

Love,
Thy Soul

When you follow your path
You will naturally shine
People will put you on a pedestal
A pedestal up so high

They will treat you as admirable
Then all of a sudden you are the bad guy
When you don't meet their expectations

They'll kick you down
Knock off your crown
Do not get mad at them
For they saw your potential

- The Universe

You do not have to
Jump off a plane or go on
a world cruise to live

You do not need to
Leap off a cliff or ice skate
If you don't want to

You just have to dare
Dare to live just a little
Live a little more

\- The Universe

There once was a god-dess full of anger
For those that put em in the path of danger.
Once the story turned tragic,
It made em apathetic.
Ey really was starting to be a believer.

Eye lost my way
Eye lost my will
Eye spin in circles
Eye can't stand still
Everything is loud
Everything is too bright
Eye can't seem to dance
Eye can't even write

Temperance

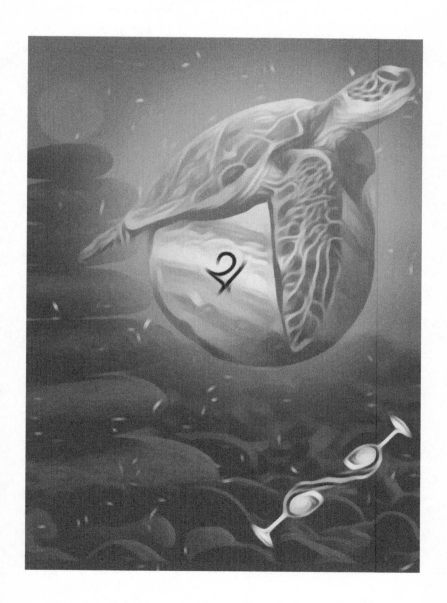

Anger is a bonfire
Keep yourself lit
So you may warm others
Don't allow it to engulf
Use your fire wisely
What are you trying
To create with it, darling
Use your love as alchemy

I've never compared myself to others,
Until other's compared themselves to me.
Turned into a public mirror,
Now I can't seem to see me
in anyone I see.

- Perhaps I finally know

Thy self

When we become
Lost and absent
of guidance
is when we are
able to experience
reality
for what it truly is
We feel the pain
The injustice
The hate

This is when you
become
your own guide
Using what we know
needs to be changed
to find
your way back
to alignment
The inevitable case
of fallen angels

we are in hell
To pay for things
We do not remember
To relearn things
Stuck in the matrix
An unwilling member

Oh *her?*
She's a nobody. She's depressed.
She is too shy to be anyone.
She needs to lose weight.
She's not really sick.
She just needs a break.
She needs to learn to
take care of herself.

Oh her?
She is ignorant of herself.
Another wannabe. Another pothead.
She doesn't even know herself.
Trying to hide from herself.

Oh her?
She is an inspiration.
A goddess. Fearless.
She is so motivational.
Everything I ever wished I could be.
She is fucking sensational.
She gives me hope.

Oh her?
She dares to have fun.
She is magic in the making.
She is connected to her higher self.
She is kind to everyone else.
She is becoming herself.
She is not afraid to be herself.

Oh her?
She is a slut. A whore.
She is a copycat.
She thinks she's all that.
She is a little obsessed with herself.
She's a fake. A gold digger.
She is an attention seeking snake.
Selfish and heartless.
She needs to be corrected.

Oh her?
She won't be around for too long.
She can't keep up the act up too long.
She let go of herself.
She's pathetic. Boring.

Oh her?
Yeah.. I knew her.
I hated her. I loved her.
I didn't believe in her.
whatever happened to her?

Her.
I... am... her.
Eye am them.
We write our story.
Not them.

The stickiness
of resistance
of feeling yourself
fighting
but the mere thought
of letting go
sinks you deeper
into the quicksand
That is when
your wings
will come in handy

Love,
Thy Soul

Ignorance is bliss
Ignorance of privilege
Ignorance of suffering
Ignoring the fire
May bring
Temporary peace
But won't
Put out the fire

Some fires are needed
The destruction
Rarely feels nourishing
Yet, everything returns
To feed the soil
For new life
To grow

Set fire to the patriarchy
Even if I get burned
I'm willing to burn
For the next generation
Us witches usually do

A spiritual practice can be very healing,
if you aren't using it to punish yourself.
Don't be afraid to feel your feelings,
so you can merge with your higher self.

I used to take offense
Offense to labels and being defined.
It made me feel misunderstood.
Now I know I am infinite;
I am everything, and I am nothing.
There is no definition of me.

I used to take offense
Then I took defense
Now, I take acceptance.

You deserve to experience all of
the love that resides within you.

The love you so graciously you give away;
Hearts broken. Friendships betrayed.

Darling, there is no need to feel blue
for any love that has bid ado.
All love resides within you.

A love letter to yourself, you will write
underneath the silver moonlight
and kiss yourself goodnight.

Wake in the morning, anew;
Making peace with all you have been through,
for you have so much loving yet to do.

Fluent range of emotions
of what you see when you don't see
Flexibility of the senses
Permeating
Beats

Excuse me
As I let go
Of those
That tell me
To let go···
Of things
My mind
Heart and soul
can hardly
grasp

Everything has meaning
Everything means nothing.
Nothing is meaning.
Meaning means nothing.

How can I expect others
not to judge me when I have
judged myself all my life?

Reluctant to judge others…
Perhaps I should have
started with my damn self.

I love myself
I am honestly starting to
I'm learning to stand on my own
But why should anyone have to

Love, Thy Soul

Take me back
Back to the skies
For dreaming sustains

Little giggles and metal toy cars
That bring me smiles
On cloudy days
I levitate us to better times
Both of the past, and those yet to come

Realigning
Surviving
Yet, to fully thrive

For what is hope
For those who have never had it

Dreaming
Dreaming is hope
In a universe,
A skip and hop away
I'll take you with me

No.

You'll take me with you, child
For your innocence and spirit
know the way...

Things tend to happen
For a reason. Sometimes, those
Reasons are shitty.

You can never not be yourself, darling
That is a lie we tell ourselves.
That we somehow must become someone else
Or some better form of our self.

That if we change, or evolve,
Ourselves we never truly were.
Not recognizing that we
are always changing,
yet always remain the same.

Our personality, a constant blur.
A mixture of experience and intentions
Our souls guiding our direction.

Sometimes we may seem lost,
when were exactly where we need to be.
Finding ourselves through synchronicity.

Spirituality is liberation
Not condemnation

Spirituality is self exploration
Spirituality is finding connection
Spirituality is awareness of perception
Spirituality is expansion

It's pursuing your passions
It's being aware of our reactions
It's about growing compassion
For self and others

Let go of calculations
Let go of expectations
Let go of limitations
Enjoy your sexual liberation
Or your celibacy
Dare to taste a new delicacy

Spirituality is free will
You are allowed to have thrills
Call off work, and fly to Brazil
Dance and make love in the kitchen
Go to a drum circle in Asheville
Whatever journey you take
Your soul, you should fulfill

Love,
Thy Soul

when you learn that not everyone
Has to, or will, like you,
You also learn that you also do not
Have to like everyone, either.

They call me beautiful,
as if it meant that I was
something special.

They call me peaceful,
as if I hadn't swallowed
My scream and shout.

They call me courageous,
as if I there was a prize to win.

They call me gentle,
as if my life hasn't beaten me
over and over, like a stone at a beach.

They call me careless,
as if I wasn't drowning
In anxieties and worries.

They call me attention seeking,
as if I begged them to watch
The orchestra they composed
And brought popcorn to.

They call me loud,
As they punch
every scream out.

They call me···
I don't answer.
I turned off
my service.

Read the energy, not the words
Listen to their soul, not their thoughts
Follow the message, not the person

-    The Universe

I begged you for death...
You show me how to live.

I asked you for love...
You taught me to love myself.

I surrendered, and
You gifted me back control.

was asking for hope,
And you mold me into hope.

was asking for connection
You took everyone away
Even you, Universe

so we found
each other along
the way

If you are thirsty,
May your glass
Be filled.

If you are hungry,
May you find
Nourishment.

If you're tired,
May your soul
Find peace.

If you're at peace,
May you find
The spark within
To create peace
For others.

When my mouth is silent,
my mind pounds with words.
When I finish writing,
Silence rests in my mind
The comforting rhythm of
emptiness,
where my soul finds peace.
Where my mind can breathe.

They tell us to love ourselves
Yet tell us to simmer down
when we do.

They want us to heal
But ignore our aches
and pains, too.

They want us not to be depressed,
anxious, or stressed, yet criticize
where compassion should
be expressed.

They want us to open our mind
Only to their flawed theories.
Freethinking group thinking.

They want us to be ourselves
But defined by their
Perceptions.

They want us to conform
To accept accusations
To fit in.

We will tear all of their
little boxes to
smithereens

Love,
Thy Soul

People who have been hurt don't hurt people.
People hurt people.

People full of love don't love people.
People love people.

Pain lives; fortunately, so does love.
So do people.

A rose never worries about it's thorns
causing pain to gentle hands.
Daisies grow without anxiety
of their gentleness or fragility.
A weed grows determined,
without worrying about being pretty.
Trees grow, without fear
of ever being cut down or burned.
A poison ivy bush grows
without shaming itself of its toxicity.
A dandelion grows,
without knowledge of the wishes it creates.
A sunflower grows,
with no care as to how tall it will become.
You are allowed to grow and become
without being afraid
of growing into yourself.

-The Universe

I was thrown off a cliff, so I became the wind.
I was drowned, so I became the water.
I was buried, so I grew into a tree.
I was cut down, so I became a shelter.
I was burnt, so I became the fire.
I was hungry, so I ate the smores.
I was satisfied, so I smiled.

Love,
Thy Soul

only love heals
Illnesses of
the spirit

Love,
Thy Soul

This journey raised me
crawling on the floor
Only to relearn
How to walk

This journey brought me to life
Holding my breath
Only to relearn
How to breathe

This journey changed me
Wanting to change my flaws
Only to learn
How to accept myself

This journey humbled me
Never enough or always too much
Only to relearn
It's not quantity or quality

It is love
It is all love

Love,
Thy Soul

we are all perfect souls masked
In human imperfections.

we are all perfect humans masked
In soul imperfections.

we are all imperfect souls masked
In human perfections.

Del Mar
Del Sol
Del cielo
De la Luna
De las estrellas
De el universo

❤

Continue your journey...

Get 369 days of self love affirmations and journal prompts!

Available at Amazon

Art : Phoebe
cover : Joanna
Editing : V.
Poems : Phoebe, Joanna, V., and X

First print edition 2020.

Disclaimer: Poetry is not to be understood, but rather to be felt. The content found within may not be suitable for every situation. May this book aid you in creating positive situations. This work is sold with the understanding that neither the author nor the publisher is held responsible for the results accrued from the advice in this book. keep reading and researching, to form your own conclusions.

10 9 8 7 6 5 4 3 2 1 0

ISBN: 978-1-7321424-4-2 (Paperback Edition)
ISBN: 978-1-7321424-3-5 (kindle Edition)

Made in the USA
Coppell, TX
30 July 2020